©LEVEL-5/YWP

YO-KAI WATCH ® : ANNUAL 2017

A CENTUM BOOK 978-1-910917-02-2

Published in Great Britain by Centum Books Ltd

Centum Books Ltd, 20 Devon Square,

Newton Abbot, Devon, TQ12 2HR, UK

books@centumbooksltd.co.uk

CENTUM BOOKS Limited Reg. No. 07641486

This edition published 2016

A CIP catalogue record for this book

is available from the British Library.

Printed in China

1 3 5 7 9 10 8 6 4 2

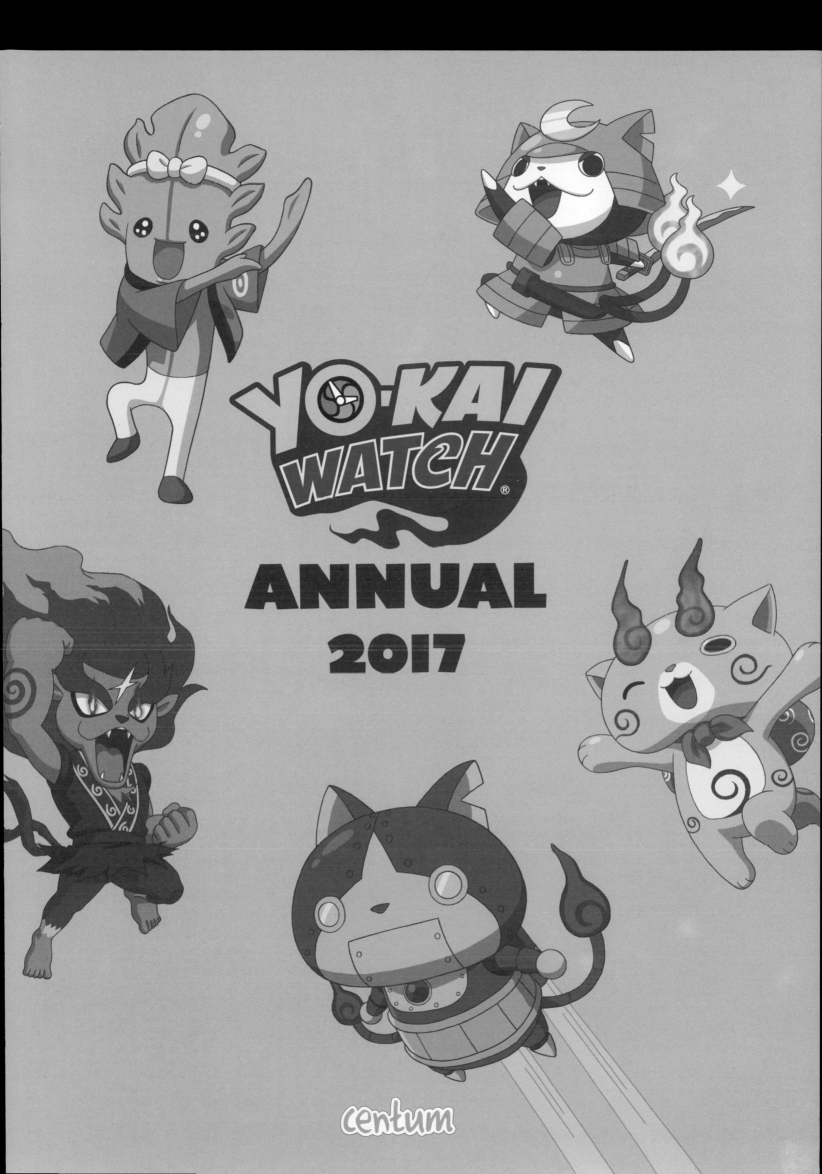

It's Yo-kai Time!

Hi there, I'm Nate. My life is pretty normal. You know, average: school, friends and fun! But then I met Whisper and he gave me this watch. Now I can see these invisible beings called Yo-kai in my everyday life.

This book will tell you all you need to know about Yo-kai, but first let me introduce you to Whisper, my self-proclaimed butler.

You'd think that being a Yo-kai would mean that Whisper knows all about his kind, but he often resorts to looking at his Yo-kai Pad.

Nate is such a kidder!

Good day to you young Yo-kai fan. I am Whisper. Yo-kai Butler and expert in all things Yo-kai.

The world of Yo-kai is fascinating so you've come to right place for all your Yo-kai needs. Colouring, doodling, facts and a plethora of puzzles are waiting for you, as well as all your favourite Yo-kai.

Plus you'll love the Yo-kai Watch press-outs, including masks, Watch, Pad and Annual Collectors Challenge Points! Find them in the middle of the book.

Are you ready?

Answers are on pages 73-77!

Collectors Challenge

To test your Yo-kai knowledge we've hidden 36 "Collectors Challenge" questions throughout the pages of this book. Answer the questions and each time you get one right award yourself a point from the press-out pieces found in the middle of the book. The answers are on page 77.

32
JIBANYAN

14
HAPPIERRE

23
HIDABAT

Your challenge is to collect as many press-out points as possible by answering all the questions correctly, then discover your expert rating on page 69.

How many points will you collect?
Here's your first question. Good luck!

Collectors Challenge
Where did Nate and Whisper first meet?

Yo-kai Basics

First up, let's learn some essential Yo-kai facts.
These are things that every Yo-kai fan needs to know.

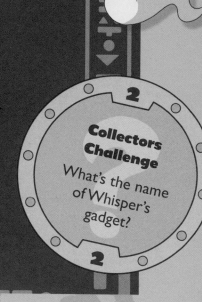

Essential Facts

- Yo-kai are beings that live in a parallel universe.
- They often come to the human realm and cause havoc and mischief.
- Yo-kai are either born from the soul of a human who has unfinished business or from an everyday object that just came to be.
- A Yo-kai Watch enables you to see the Yo-kai.
- If you make friends with a Yo-kai, then you can collect their medal.
- Summon a Yo-kai using their medal and they will help you in any way they can (depending on their mood)!
- Yo-kai belong to different tribes. Members of the same tribe share similar qualities or characteristics.
- Each tribe has a symbol. Learn them below.

Collectors Challenge
What's the name of Whisper's gadget?

2   2

The Tribes

Work out the tribe names by unscrambling the letters.

1) B A R V E

_ _ _ _ _

2) M I N G H A R C

_ _ _ _ _ _ _ _

3) I S E T O U R M Y S

_ _ _ _ _ _ _ _ _ _

4) F U L A R T H E

_ _ _ _ _ _ _ _

5) Y A D H S

_ _ _ _ _

6) E E E I R

_ _ _ _ _

7) P P L I S E R Y

_ _ _ _ _ _ _ _

8) G T O U H

_ _ _ _ _

Brave Tribe

These Yo-kai are best in battle and have brave characteristics. They fill humans with a fighting energy whenever they are nearby. Now read about some members of this tribe.

BLAZION

The king of beasts with a mane of fire! A hot-headed lion Yo-kai with the ability to fire people up.

ALL ABOUT BLAZION:

Ability: Makes people feel competitive

Unique Trait: He has fire burning in his heart . . . and eyes . . . and hair.

Secret: He's a martial arts expert.

Mantra: Freeloaders and slackers get nowhere in life.

SHEEN

This swordsman is a martial arts master who battles with the power of wind and lightning on his side.

ALL ABOUT SHEEN:

Ability: Lightning swordsmanship

Unique Trait: His swordsman's hat

Secret to his Power: His legendary blade

Back Story: His spirit was reignited by a legendary blade.

B3-NKı

B3-NKı is half machine and he can use his pole arm to pierce through technological devices making them break.

ALL ABOUT B3-NKı:

Ability: Breaks machines to collect screws

Unique Trait: Loves his sword

Mission: To collect his 100th screw to make his sword awesome!

Secret: He thinks Robonyan is a weirdo!

SHOGUNYAN

The spirit of Jibanyan's ancestor, Shogunyan is a legendary Yo-kai. Not much is known about him except that he is an adorable samurai sword master.

ALL ABOUT SHOGUNYAN:

Ability: Mad samurai-sword skills

Backstory: He's Jibanyan's Yo-kai ancestor.

Signature Style: Always has a samurai sword at his waist

Loves: Cake – the ancient version of chocobars

Charming Tribe

Charming Yo-kai are the cutest of all. However, they are very mischievous and love sweet things. Now read about some of members of this tribe.

JIBANYAN

Jibanyan used to be a real cat . . . until a mishap with a truck made him a Yo-kai.

ALL ABOUT JIBANYAN:

Ability: Inspirits people to walk into traffic

Loves: Chocobars and taking naps

Favourite Girl Band: Next HarMEOWny

Catchphrase: "I'm busy right nyow." / "What is it nyow, Nyate?"

KOMAJIRO

Komajiro is Komasan's little brother, and he admires his big bro more than anyone in the whole wide Yo-kai world!

ALL ABOUT KOMAJIRO:

Ability: Why, he wouldn't inspirit a person any more than snow would fall in summertime!

Mission: To learn all about life in the big city.

Personal Hero: Komasan, of course

Catchphrase: "Oh, big brother, lookie here!"

KOMASAN

This harmless country bumpkin is a big softie with a weakness for ice cream. Don't we all?

ALL ABOUT KOMASAN:

Ability: Steals a lick of people's ice cream

Speaks with: A country accent

Likes: Writing home to Mama

Catchphrase: "Oh my swirls!"

WALKAPPA

Walkappa's a pretty laid-back dude. This Yo-kai is slick at defusing confrontations.

ALL ABOUT WALKAPPA:

Ability: Makes people chill out

Looks Like: A duck-dude with a plate on his head

Favourite Food: Enjoys pizza, man

Catchphrase: "Totally bogus, man."

Eerie Tribe

There's something not quite right about Yo-kai from the Eerie tribe. They love to hide around corners, creep people out, and either drive you insane or into a pit of gloom. Now read about some of members of this tribe.

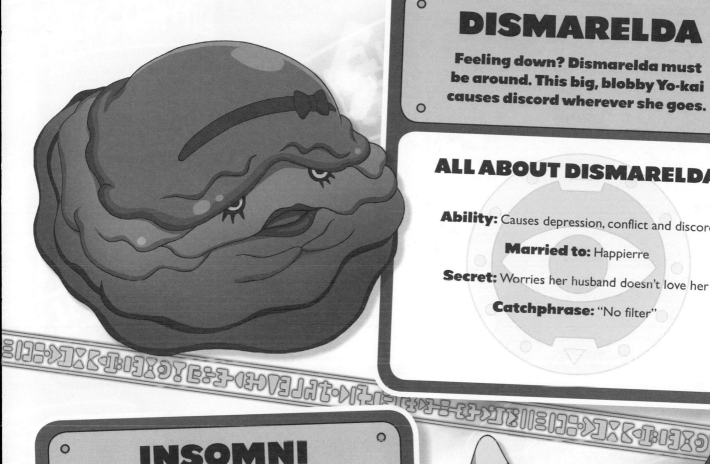

DISMARELDA

Feeling down? Dismarelda must be around. This big, blobby Yo-kai causes discord wherever she goes.

ALL ABOUT DISMARELDA:

Ability: Causes depression, conflict and discord

Married to: Happierre

Secret: Worries her husband doesn't love her

Catchphrase: "No filter"

INSOMNI

Insomni is the stuff of nightmares. She enjoys keeping people awake all night so they fall asleep during the day.

ALL ABOUT INSOMNI:

Ability: Keeps people awake

Unique Trait: Only needs one contact lens

Secret: Can fall asleep

Greatest Foe: Baku

MANJIMUTT

Poor Manjimutt. He's neither a man nor an adorable puppy: he's a sad mix of the two, with a self-worth complex to boot.

ALL ABOUT MANJIMUTT:

Ability: Makes people share his misery

What Is He?: Man + Toy Poodle x Wood = MANJIMUTT

Favourite Drink: Toilet water

Dreams of: Becoming a CEO!

CHEEKSQUEEK

Stinky doesn't begin to cut it when it comes to Cheeksqueek's cheese-cutting capabilities. This foul-smelling Yo-kai makes people fart unexpectedly.

ALL ABOUT CHEEKSQUEEK:

Ability: Makes people toot

Responsible for: The Great Flatulence Pandemic of 2007

Looks Like: A giant bottom

Catchphrase: "Poo-poo!"

Heartful Tribe

This tribe of Yo-kai are geared towards helping and healing – from changing a mood for the better, to filling your belly with yummy food. These guys are generally good to have around. Now read about some of members of this tribe.

HAPPIERRE

This cheery Yo-kai emanates warmth and happiness wherever he goes.

ALL ABOUT HAPPIERRE:

Ability: Makes people feel happy

Married to: Dismarelda

Motto: Ze French way is ze happy way.

Speaks with: A French accent

SEAWEED TRIO

These Yo-kai will always make sure you are in the mood for dancing, even when there's no beat to dance to!

ALL ABOUT THE SEAWEED TRIO:

Ability: They make people dance ... a LOT.

Look Like: Wiggly pieces of seaweed

Secret: You can't stop the beat when it's in your soul.

Catchphrase: "Dance like no one's watching!"

Mysterious Tribe

The Yo-kai of this tribe surround themselves in a shroud of mystery. Strange appearances and strange sorcery are at work. Now read about some of members of this tribe.

KYUBI

Kyubi is an elite master of fire who can make volcanoes erupt. He wants to collect his 100th heart in order to be promoted.

ALL ABOUT KYUBI:

Ability: Transformation

Unique Trait: His long fingernails

Mission: To collect his 100th heart

Mantra: In the game of love there's move and counter-move.

TATTLETELL

This Yo-kai will make you reveal your innermost secrets and the more embarrassing they are the better!

ALL ABOUT TATTLETELL:

Ability: Forces people to reveal their innermost secrets

Worst Secret Spilled: Let's just say it involved a trip to the bathroom.

Enjoys: A good cup of tea and a chat.

Catchphrase: "Tattle-tellllllllll!"

Tough Tribe

These Yo-kai boast high defenses due to their dense bodies and stubborn spirit. Now read about some of members of this tribe.

ROBONYAN

Robonyan is a robotic version of Jibanyan from the future. or at least, he says he is. Either way, he's one tough kitty!

ALL ABOUT ROBONYAN:

Ability: He is the ultimate robot Yo-kai.

Back-to-the-Future Story: He's a robotic version of Jibanyan from the future.

Secret: He has a built-in chocobar factory.

Mission: Unknown

NOWAY

Noway has a way of turning your life upside down. Want to go to a party? No way. That's how Noway rolls.

ALL ABOUT NOWAY:

Ability: Makes people say "no way" to everything

Secret: Just wants a friend, but everyone keeps saying "no way."

Looks Like: A wall

Catchphrase: "No Way" (obviously)

Slippery Tribe

These independent, free-thinking spirits have slimy, snake-like features. It's hard to grab these guys! Now read about some of members of this tribe.

SPENP

Hold on tight to your wallet, because when Spenp is around, there's no telling how he'll make your allowance disappear.

ALL ABOUT SPENP:

Ability: Makes people spend all their money on silly stuff

Backstory: He's a change purse from the yuppie era of the 1980s.

Likes: Shopping sprees

Catchphrase: "I work hard and I play hard."

VENOCT

The mysterious and elite Venoct has an incredible amount of power. Little is known about him, apart from that he uses his living dragon scarf as a weapon.

ALL ABOUT VENOCT:

Ability: Unknown

Unique Trait: Unknown

Secret: Unknown

Mantra: Unknown

Shady Tribe

These dark-hearted Yo-kai often bring out
the worst behaviour in nearby humans.
Read about Hidabat!

HIDABAT

Hidabat is a Yo-kai that lurks in the
shadows, possessing people and
convincing them to lock themselves
away from the rest of the world.

ALL ABOUT HIDABAT:

Ability: Makes people lock themselves away

Can Be Found in: Caves, closets, under beds

Not-So-Secret Secret: Everything frightens him.

Trademark: Emits ultrasonic waves that
only Yo-kai can hear

Favourite Yo-kai

Who is your favourite Yo-kai? Write about your favourite below
and give three reasons as to why you think they are best.

My favourite Yo-kai is:

1

2

3

Tribe Match It!

Were you paying attention? Let's find out.
Match the Yo-kai to their tribes.

BRAVE

CHARMING

MYSTERIOUS

SLIPPERY

EERIE

TOUGH

HEARTFUL

SHADY

TATTLETELL

HIDABAT

HAPPIERRE

SPENP

BLAZION

INSOMNI

WALKAPPA

NOWAY

Collectors Challenge

3

What did Walkappa reveal he loves to eat during an encounter with Tattletell?

3

Yo-kai Yourself!

Imagine if you were a Yo-kai. What characteristics would best describe you?
Would you be mischievous? Would you get people fired up like Blazion?
Or would you be something completely different?

Write your top five characteristics below:

1 ....

2 ....

3 ....

4 ....

5 ....

Create your Yo-kai name and write it in this box:

....

What's your story?

....

....

....

Now design your Yo-kai Medal:

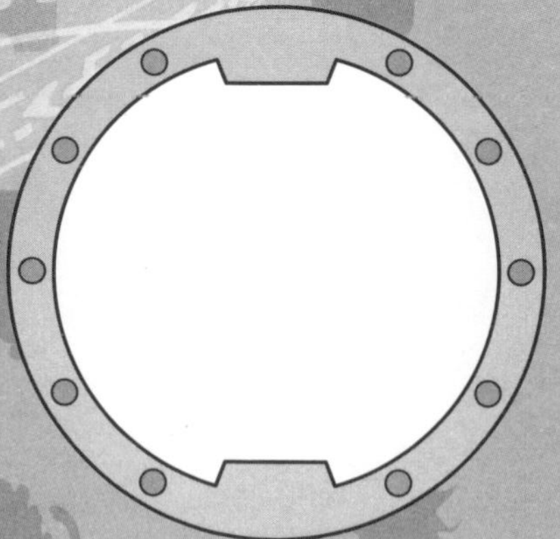

What tribe would you belong to, or would you create a new one? Write about it here:

....

....

Now it's time to draw yourself as a Yo-kai!

How many eyes would you have?

Will you have claws and jaws?

Will you have fur or skin?

Will you look friendly or scary?

Collectors Challenge

Who is also known as the "man-faced dog"?

Brothers Re-united

Komajiro has become lost in the big city. Find a path through the maze and help him get back to his big brother, Komasan.

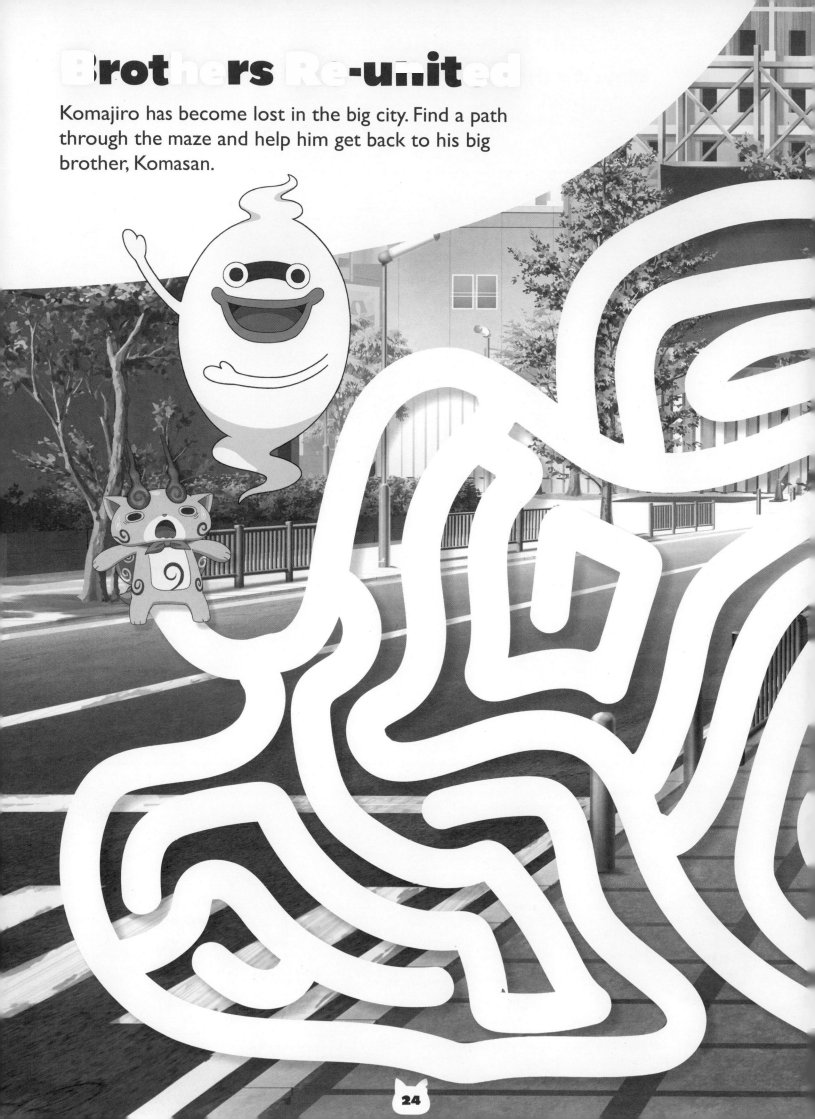

Colour Jibanyan

Use your most charming colours to complete this picture of Jibanyan!

Collectors Challenge

6

Who hangs out at service stations making people hungry?

6

Broken Image

B3-NK1 has messed around with Whisper's Yo-kai Pad and now it's not displaying ANYTHING correctly. Can you piece the broken parts of this picture back together to work out who is in the picture?

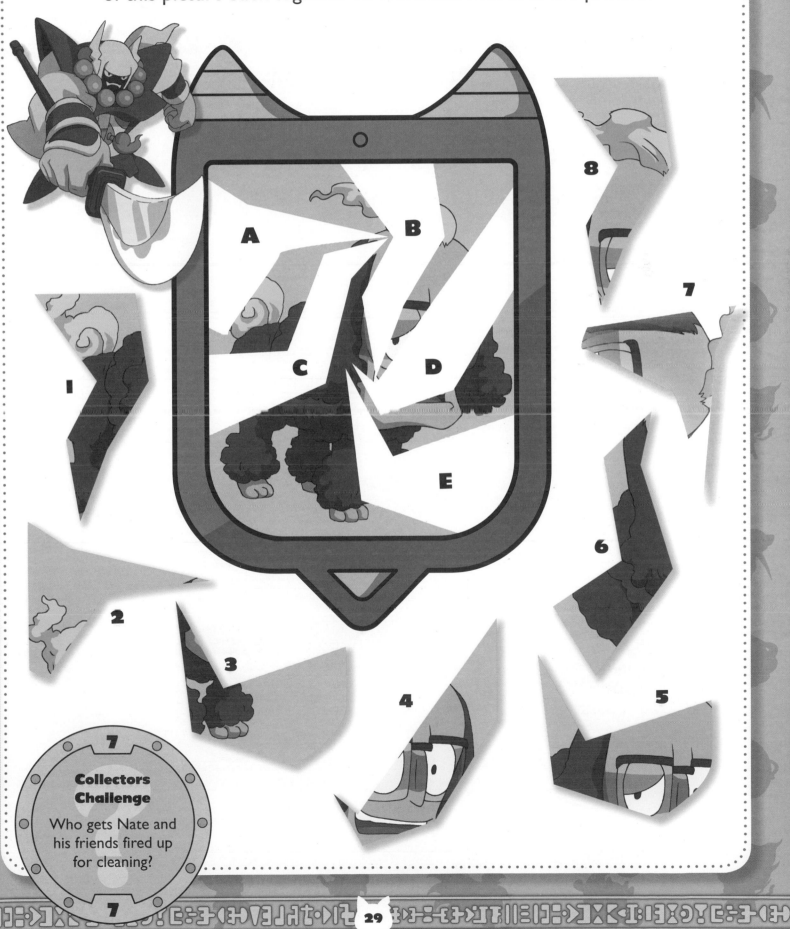

A

B

C

D

E

8

7

1

2

3

4

5

6

7

Collectors Challenge

Who gets Nate and his friends fired up for cleaning?

7

Whisper's Wise Words

There are three things that Whisper thinks are worth fighting for.
Use the code below to work out what they are!

A	B	C	D	E	F	G	H	I	J	K	L	M
10	9	3	4	17	24	23	25	26	5	22	12	16

N	O	P	Q	R	S	T	U	V	W	X	Y	Z
18	6	15	11	21	8	20	7	14	1	13	2	19

___ ___ ___ ___ ___   ___ ___ ___ ___ ___ ___ ___
20 21 7   20 25   5   7   8   20 26 3   17

___ ___ ___   ___ ___ ___ ___ ___ ___
10 18 4   21 17 10 12 12 2

___ ___ ___ ___   ___ ___ ___ ___ ___ ___
23 6   6   4   18 10 3   25 6   8

8

Collectors Challenge

What's the name of the Yo-kai trio who disrupt the school exams?

8

Yo-kai Only

Everyone needs a bit of privacy now and again to concentrate on studying Yo-kai, so cut out the sign and put it on your bedroom door.

9

Collectors Challenge

What does Manjimutt want to go to Hollywood for?

9

KEEP OUT!
THERE'S YO-KAI ABOUT

YO-KAI EXPERTS ONLY!

1

NATE

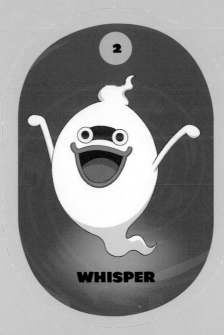

2

WHISPER

3

YO-KAI WATCH

4

BEAR

5

EDDIE

6

KATIE

7

YO-KAI PAD

8

ROUGHRAFF

9

FIDGEPHANT

11

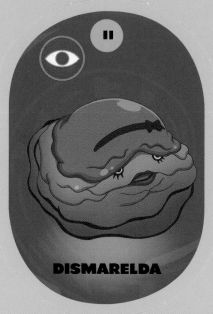

DISMARELDA

12

INSOMNI

13

MANJIMUTT

14

HAPPIERRE

15

HUNGRAMPS

16

SEAWEED TRIO

17

SHOGUNYAN

18

WAZZAT

19
KYUBI

20
TATTLETELL

21
NEGATIBUZZ

22
DIMMY

23
HIDABAT

24
NOKO

25
SPENP

26
VENOCT

27
ROBONYAN

28

CHEEKSQUEEK

YO·KAI WATCH®

30
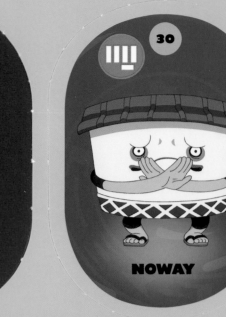
NOWAY

YO·KAI WATCH®

32

JIBANYAN

33

KOMAJIRO

34

KOMASAN

35

WALKAPPA

36

BADDINYAN

Medal Code

Count the number of each medal type below. Then complete Nate's famous phrase by writing the letters over each number and solving the code.

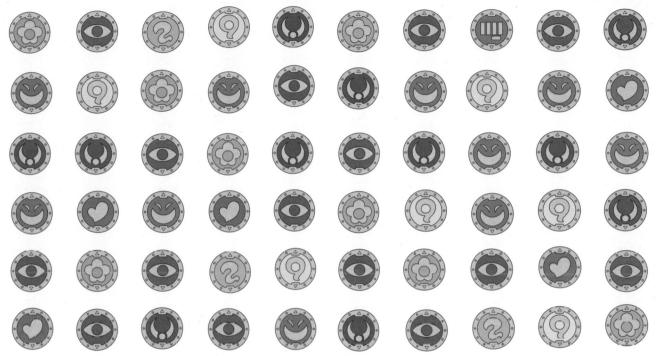

How many did you count?

⬤	II	G	✿		O
◉		H	😈		A
▦		M	👁		D
♥		E	〜		Y

_ _-K_I _ _ _ _L, _ _
3 8   10   1 5 15 10   15 8

_ _UR T_IN _!
3 8   7   11

Colour Blazion

It's time to get fired up as you colour in Blazion using your fiercest colours!

Collectors Challenge

Where do Komasan and Komajiro come from?

EERIE

HEARTFUL

In the Shadows

The Shady Yo-kai love lurking in the shadows. Can you work out which shadow matches the Yo-kai in each column?

12
Collectors Challenge
Who causes a huge queue for the toilet?
12

Happy Doodles

When Happierre's around, he'll definitely lift your mood and even give you happy thoughts. Doodle the top five things that make you happy in the circles below.

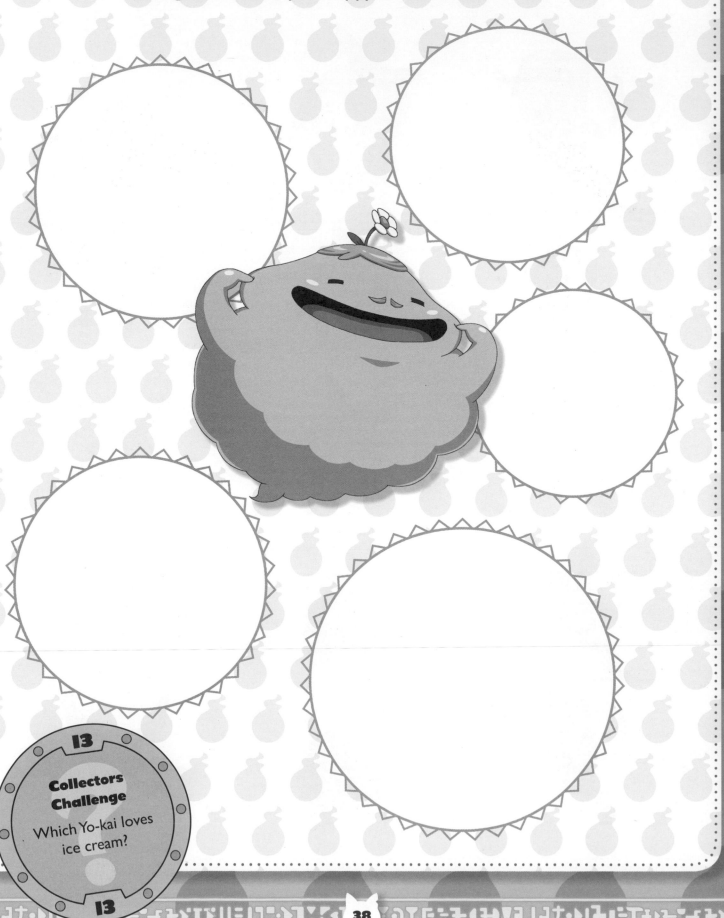

Collectors Challenge

Which Yo-kai loves ice cream?

13

13

Feeling Gloomy

When Dismarelda's around, you will feel very glum indeed. Can work out the order of the pieces of the picture below?

14

Collectors Challenge

Which Yo-kai looks a bit like purple jelly?

14

1 2 3 4 5 6 7 8

Correct Order

_ _ _ _ _ _ _ _

Yo-kai-doku!

Solve these Yo-kai-doku puzzles by making sure each Yo-kai only appears in each row, column and mini square once. Colour in the squares to complete the puzzles.

Collectors Challenge

15

15

What must Walkappa do so he can go on his daily strolls?

C

D

16

Collectors Challenge

Who wears dragons around their neck?

16

Dance With Me!

The Yo-kai dancers make anyone dance for no reason at all — even when there's no music! Can you find all the dance related words in the grid below?

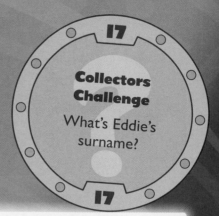
17

Collectors Challenge

What's Eddie's surname?

17

L	O	W	C	S	Y	H	R	G	A	A	E	G	Y	D
V	Y	H	F	L	P	K	P	U	N	K	I	U	F	T
T	Z	P	L	R	B	V	N	D	O	M	B	F	K	R
A	W	D	O	H	T	G	Y	H	N	U	A	L	O	O
P	B	W	A	Q	S	D	T	C	V	T	L	N	B	J
I	R	K	D	S	A	M	B	A	Q	A	L	Z	O	O
T	E	R	E	S	L	A	S	C	U	I	E	G	L	V
X	A	R	T	D	S	W	A	T	Y	C	T	M	L	O
I	K	K	J	Y	A	T	R	F	D	E	S	A	Y	C
P	D	H	Y	F	I	O	J	T	J	D	S	D	W	U
W	A	L	T	Z	F	D	T	S	T	A	N	G	O	J
F	N	P	L	L	A	W	X	T	V	B	U	I	O	S
A	C	E	D	I	S	C	O	V	V	V	X	P	D	L
A	E	A	W	C	T	S	D	F	U	I	V	C	A	U
A	S	W	E	T	Y	B	U	H	R	H	M	P	S	F

SAMBA

BALLET

WALTZ

TANGO

TAP

SALSA

DISCO

BREAKDANCE

BOLLYWOOD

PUNK

Shady Snaps

There's something different in each of these Shady photos. Look at picture **A**, then compare it to **B**, **C** and **D**. See if you can find a tiny difference in each picture. Circle the differences.

18

Collectors Challenge

Who makes you tell the truth?

18

A

B

C

D

Colour Kyubi

Think you've got what it takes to colour in this all-powerful Yo-kai?

19

Collectors Challenge

What's the first medal Nate collects?

19

Dot-to-dot

Connect the dots to reveal a legendary Yo-kai!

Collectors Challenge

Who does Nate have a crush on?

20
20

Medal Mayhem

Baddinyan loves mess and loves making a mess – he thinks it's cool. He has messed up Nate's Yo-kai Medals and now they are everywhere!

Start

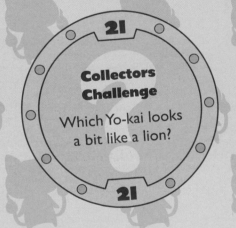

21

Collectors Challenge

Which Yo-kai looks a bit like a lion?

21

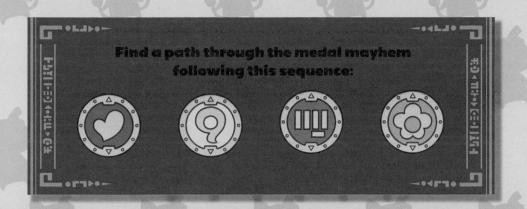

Find a path through the medal mayhem following this sequence:

22

Collectors Challenge

Which Yo-kai stops Nate from saying yes to Katie's party invitation?

22

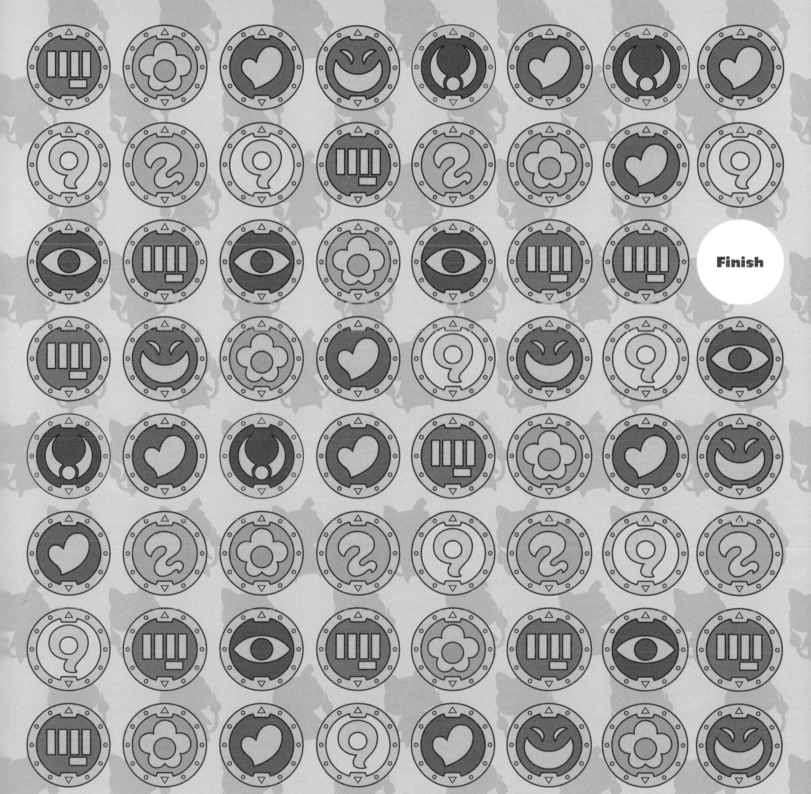

Finish

In the Mix

Can you re-order the mixed up tiles below to reveal a sentence from the Yo-kai Watch song? Then sing the lyrics if you know them.

| YOU | VER | CA | KAI |

| ME | YWH | AR | NG |

| R | H | USI | YOU | OBL |

| YO- | | | E E | | ERE |

| | | NG | | PR | EMS |

| | SSI | | UP | | AIR |

23

Collectors Challenge

Which gloomy Yo-kai looks a bit like a mosquito?

23

48

Memory Training

Feeling forgetful? Then maybe Wazzat's been messing with your memory! Test your memory skills by studying this picture for one minute, then turn over the page to answer the questions.

Memory Training

Answer these true or false questions, and then check your answers:

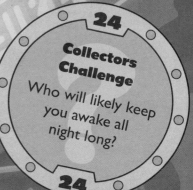

24
Collectors Challenge
Who will likely keep you awake all night long?
24

1
There were four Yo-kai Medals.

....

6
Walkappa was waving his left arm.

....

2
The Yo-kai Watch was open.

....

7
Dismarelda was not in the picture.

....

3
Whisper was next to Blazion.

....

8
The Yo-kai Pad was in Whisper's right hand.

....

4
Jibanyan's mouth was closed.

....

9
One of the medals featured Jibanyan.

....

5
Hungramps was holding a teapot.

....

10
Komajiro and Komasan were next to one another.

....

How did you score?

0-3: Wazzat is definitely messing with your memory – keep on training!

4-7: Wazzat is trying his hardest, but you're mastering your memory skills.

8-10: You're the memory champion!

Colour Walkappa

Colour in this easy-going Yo-kai in your sweetest colours!

25

Collectors Challenge

Which Yo-kai can see into the future?

25

Yo-kai Hunt

Nate is sure there's a Yo-kai up to no good, but where is it? Follow the directions and move through the grid to find out.

North

West   East

South

Directions

Start in the square labelled S, and then move:

West 3

North 6

South 1

West 3

South 6

East 2

South 1

West 5

North 8

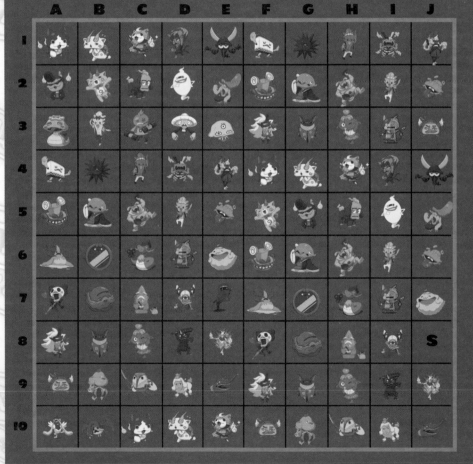

26

Collectors Challenge

Which tribe brings out the worst behaviour in humans?

26

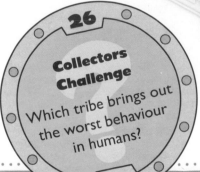

MYSTERIOUS

SHADY

Dazzabel Doodles

What crazy outfit is Dazzabel making Nate think is a good idea to wear today? Doodle your most outlandish fashion designs in the boxes to create an outfit from your nightmares!

Horrid Hat:

Terrifying Top:

Bleurgh Bag:

Terrible Trousers:

Scary Shoes:

Colour Venoct

Feel the power of the dragon as you colour in this first-class Yo-kai!

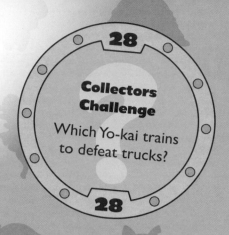

28

Collectors Challenge

Which Yo-kai trains to defeat trucks?

28

Snack Time!

Jibanyan is a Yo-kai with an appetite! He loves to snack – especially on chocobars from Nate's kitchen. Can you find all the sweet-related words in the grid below?

M	A	R	S	H	M	A	L	L	O	W	S	X	E	P	S
W	B	E	A	O	H	Y	S	P	Y	C	T	H	O	C	P
D	O	U	C	N	J	C	U	I	T	F	O	Z	L	E	M
M	A	R	P	E	N	Y	C	H	E	S	F	A	P	M	X
P	O	D	S	Y	N	E	T	T	Q	U	F	S	E	Y	C
P	L	E	A	S	C	H	S	D	F	S	E	S	D	F	S
T	U	Y	C	H	O	C	O	L	A	T	E	V	C	A	K
N	U	X	O	A	P	L	E	A	D	F	B	T	S	D	V
E	B	M	O	L	L	D	O	U	G	H	N	U	T	S	O
E	I	O	K	C	E	E	P	L	S	A	N	D	P	L	E
F	S	P	I	P	A	I	J	F	O	A	F	B	N	K	B
A	C	C	E	C	H	O	A	M	C	A	R	A	M	E	L
C	U	R	A	M	E	A	K	E	A	P	L	E	S	Y	C
L	I	O	O	P	A	N	C	A	K	E	S	T	O	F	P
P	T	A	N	C	A	K	E	S	E	H	O	C	A	S	L
M	S	R	S	H	M	A	L	T	U	M	P	L	E	P	S

CHOCOLATE   **DOUGHNUTS**

COOKIE   **CAKE**

TOFFEE   **BISCUITS**

CARAMEL   **PANCAKES**

MARSHMALLOWS   **HONEY**

29

Collectors Challenge

Which Yo-kai is a legendary ancestor of Jibanyan?

29

Outta My Way, Noway!

Noway's been causing trouble and now Nate is late for Katie's BBQ party. Find a path through the maze and don't bump into Noway!

Collectors Challenge

30

Who is a martial arts sword master?

30

58

Crazy Close-ups

Can you use your detective skills and work out who these Yo-kai are from their close-ups?

1.

3.

2.

4.

6.

5.

7.

Crossword Crackdown!

It's time to call on Blazion and get fired up to crack this tough crossword puzzle. Solve the clues below.

Across

4. The item Nate collects when he befriends a Yo-kai.

5. The name of the self-proclaimed Yo-kai butler.

7. Whisper's gadget is called this.

9. The name of Jibanyan's samurai ancestor.

Down

1. What does Nate use to detect Yo-kai?

2. Barnaby's lovable nickname.

3. What does each Yo-kai belong to?

6. The Yo-kai that comes to live with Nate and Whisper.

8. The name of Nate's crush.

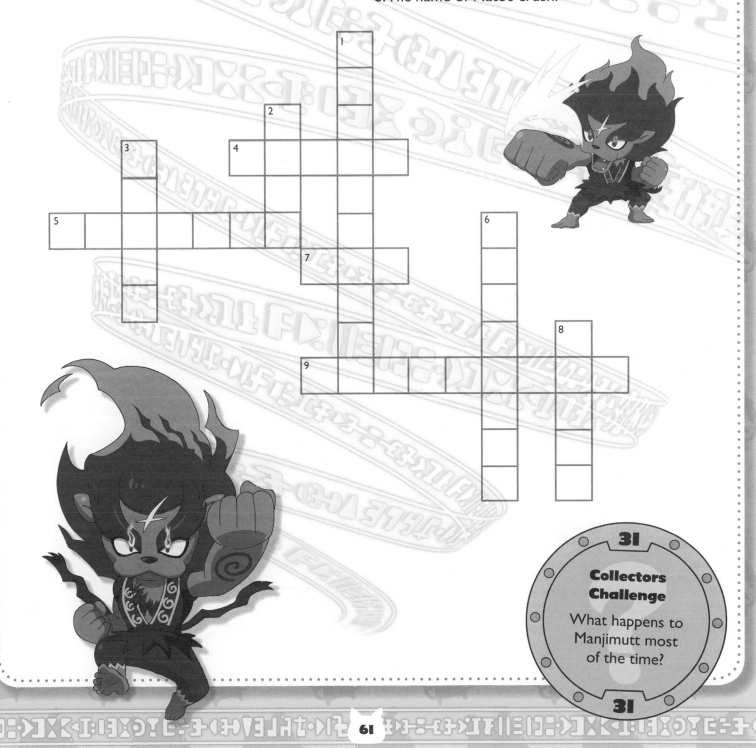

31

Collectors Challenge

What happens to Manjimutt most of the time?

31

Yo-kai Battles

Who do you think would win in these Yo-kai battles? Check their stats then see if you can work out the winners like only a true Yo-kai expert can.

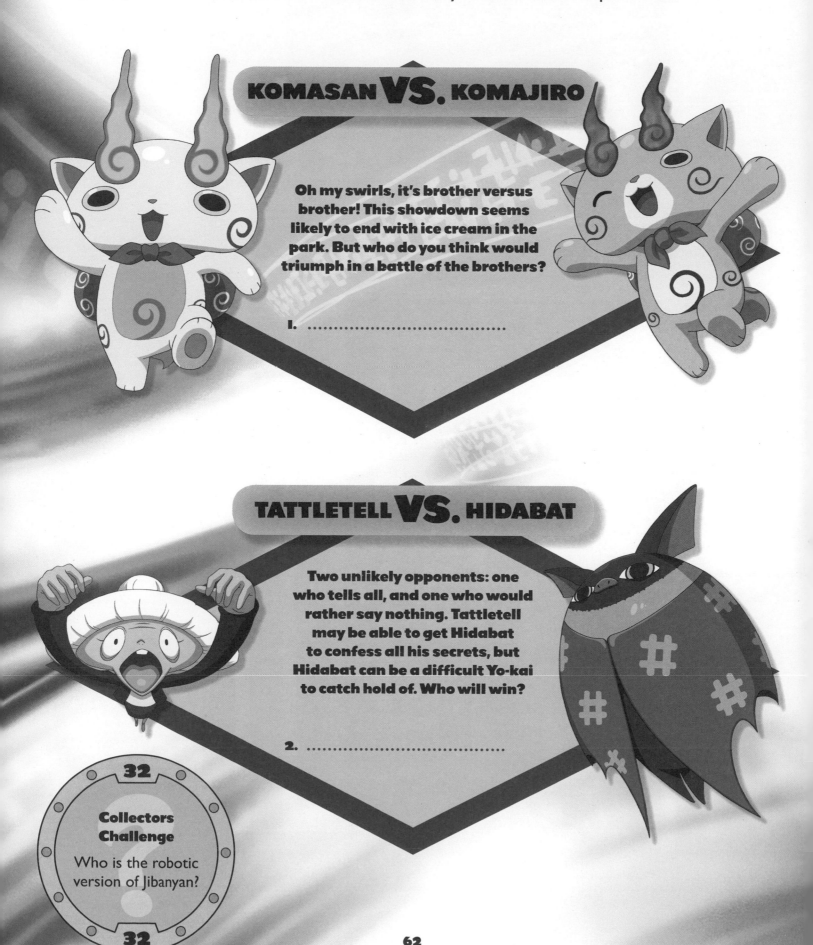

KOMASAN VS. KOMAJIRO

Oh my swirls, it's brother versus brother! This showdown seems likely to end with ice cream in the park. But who do you think would triumph in a battle of the brothers?

1. ....

TATTLETELL VS. HIDABAT

Two unlikely opponents: one who tells all, and one who would rather say nothing. Tattletell may be able to get Hidabat to confess all his secrets, but Hidabat can be a difficult Yo-kai to catch hold of. Who will win?

2. ....

Collectors Challenge

Who is the robotic version of Jibanyan?

32

32

33

Collectors Challenge

Who is married to Happiere?

33

JIBANYAN **VS.** MANJIMUTT

Jibanyan unleashes Paws of Fury, but Manjimutt disarms him with a depressing heart-to-heart. Both Yo-kai have sad backstories. Will this matchup end in flying fists or tearful hugs?

3. ....

BLAZION **VS.** WALKAPPA

Fire versus water: a formidable matchup. Blazion comes charging at Walkappa with fists blazing. But will Walkappa's go-with-the-flow attitude rain on Blazion's firestorm parade?

4. ....

Yo-kai Art

It's time to channel your creative skills into drawing these Yo-kai. Use the grids to help create your very own masterpieces.

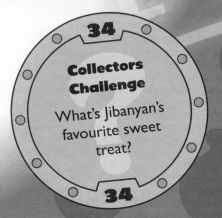

HUNGRAMPS

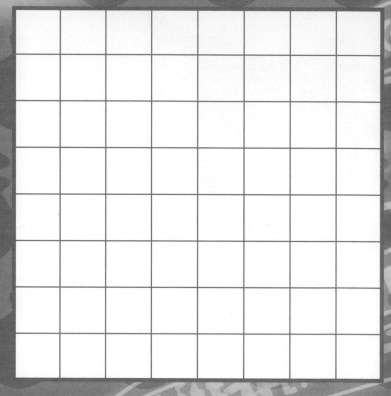

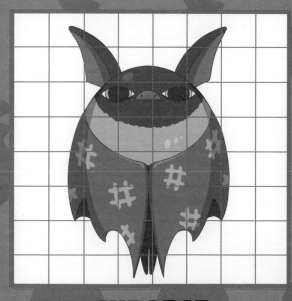

HIDABAT

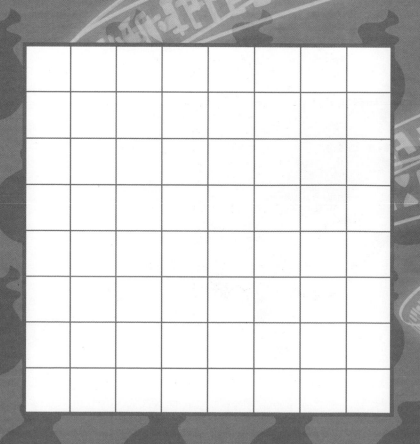

DAZZABEL

SHOGUNYAN

Word Detective

How many new words can you make from Yo-kai Watch! Try and find 30 and write them on the lines below.

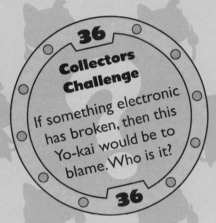

Collectors Challenge

36

If something electronic has broken, then this Yo-kai would be to blame. Who is it?

36

YO-KAI WATCH

1	11	21 ....
2	12	22 ....
3	13	23 ....
4	14	24 ....
5	15	25 ....
6	16	26 ....
7	17	27 ....
8	18	28 ....
9	19	29 ....
10	20	30 ....

SLIPPERY

TOUGH

Annual Collectors Challenge Results

How many points did you collect through the book?
Count up your press-out point pieces, then find out your expert
rating below. Are you an beginner or an expert?

0 to 5 Points: Beginner Knowledge

If you collected up to 5 points, then you've still got a lot of
work to do to raise your Yo-kai game. In the world of Yo-kai,
knowledge really is power.

6 to 15 Points: Intermediate Knowledge

You're definitely starting to get the hang of things. All you need
to do is give yourself that extra push – perhaps it's time you
called on Blazion to get you fired up for this task.

16 to 25 Points: Expert Knowledge

Wow, you're really creating a Yo-kai library of knowledge in
that head of yours – in fact you're almost like a living, breathing,
walking, talking Yo-kai encyclopaedia. Congrats!

26 to 35 Points: Master Knowledge

If there's a Yo-kai problem then you know how to solve it
- no problem. There's not much that fazes you when it
comes to Yo-kai. You can easily call yourself an expert.

36 Points: Legend

What can we say? You're simply a Yo-kai legend. Matched
only by Whisper (or his Yo-kai pad!) in knowledge.

Yo-kai Seek and Find!

This picture is packed with Yo-kai. If you look closely you'll see there are twenty-two Yo-kai medals hidden here. Can you find them all?

70

Colour Dazzabel

Use all of your style knowledge when you colour in this catwalk catastrophe!

ANSWERS

Page 8

The Tribes

1) BRAVE
2) CHARMING
3) MYSTERIOUS
4) HEARTFUL
5) SHADY
6) EERIE
7) SLIPPERY
8) TOUGH

Page 20

Tribe Match It!

SPENP	SLIPPERY
NOWAY	TOUGH
HIDABAT	SHADY
TATTLETELL	MYSTERIOUS
HAPPIERRE	HEARTFUL
INSOMNI	EERIE
WALKAPPA	CHARMING

Page 24-25

Brothers Reunited

Page 29

Broken Image

A = 2   C = 6   E = 3

B = 8   D = 4

Page 30

Whisper's Wise Words

TRUTH JUSTICE AND REALLY GOOD NACHOS

Page 33

Medal Code

O = 8 (heartful medals)
A = 10 (shady medals)
E = 5 (charming medals)
Y = 3 (slippery medals)
H = 7 (mysterious medals)
G = 11 (brave medals)
D = 15 (eerie medals)
M = 1 (tough medal)

Yo-kai medal, do your thing!

Page 37

In the Shadows

ANSWERS

Page 39

Feeling Gloomy

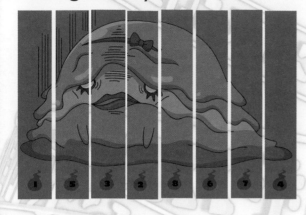

1 5 3 2 8 6 7 4

Page 40-41

Yo-kai-doku

A

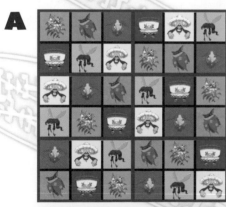

B

C

D

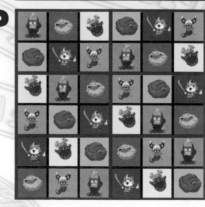

Page 42

Dance With Me!

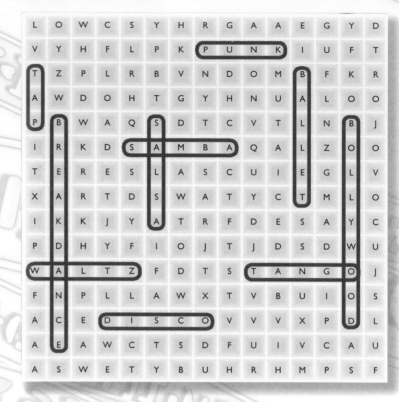

L	O	W	C	S	Y	H	R	G	A	A	E	G	Y	D
V	Y	H	F	L	P	K	P	U	N	K	I	U	F	T
T	Z	P	L	R	B	V	N	D	O	M	B	F	K	R
A	W	D	O	H	T	G	Y	H	N	U	A	L	O	O
P	B	W	A	Q	S	D	T	C	V	T	L	N	B	J
I	R	K	D	S	A	M	B	A	Q	A	L	Z	O	O
T	E	R	E	S	L	A	S	C	U	I	E	G	L	V
X	A	R	T	D	S	W	A	T	Y	C	T	M	L	C
I	K	K	J	Y	A	T	R	F	D	E	S	A	Y	C
P	D	H	Y	F	I	O	J	T	J	D	S	D	W	U
W	A	L	T	Z	F	D	T	S	T	A	N	G	O	J
F	N	P	L	L	A	W	X	T	V	B	U	I	O	S
A	C	E	D	I	S	C	O	V	V	V	X	P	D	L
A	E	A	W	C	T	S	D	F	U	I	V	C	A	U
A	S	W	E	T	Y	B	U	H	R	H	M	P	S	F

Page 43

Shady Snaps

B

C

D

Medal Mayhem

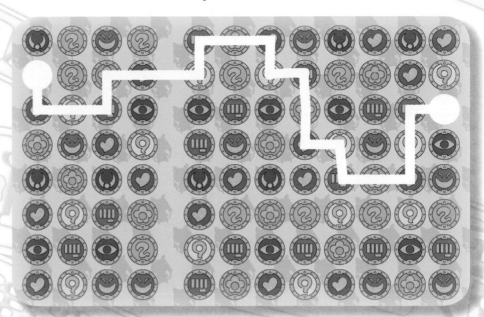

Page 48

In the Mix

YO-	KAI	AR	E	E	VER	YWH	ERE
CA	USI	NG	YOU	PR	OBL	EMS
ME	SSI	NG	UP	YOU	R	H	AIR

Page 45

Dot-to-dot

Yo-kai are everywhere
Causing you problems
messing up your hair

Page 49-50

Memory Training

1) FALSE	5) FALSE	9) TRUE
2) TRUE	6) FALSE	10) TRUE
3) FALSE	7) TRUE	
4) FALSE	8) TRUE	

It's Shogunyan!

ANSWERS

Page 51

Yo-kai Hunt

BADDINYAN is the Yo-kai up to no good in square A2.

Page 57

Snack Time!

M	A	R	S	H	M	A	L	L	O	W	S	X	E	P	S
W	B	E	A	O	H	Y	S	P	Y	C	T	H	O	C	P
D	O	U	C	N	J	C	U	I	T	F	O	Z	L	E	M
M	A	R	P	E	N	Y	C	H	E	S	F	A	P	M	X
P	O	D	S	Y	N	E	T	T	Q	U	F	S	E	Y	C
P	L	E	A	S	C	H	S	D	F	S	E	S	D	F	S
T	U	Y	C	H	O	C	O	L	A	T	E	V	C	A	K
N	U	X	O	A	P	L	E	A	D	F	B	T	S	D	V
E	B	M	O	L	L	D	O	U	G	H	N	U	T	S	O
E	I	O	K	C	E	E	P	L	S	A	N	D	P	L	E
F	S	P	I	P	A	I	J	F	O	A	F	B	N	K	B
A	C	C	E	C	H	O	A	M	C	A	R	A	M	E	L
C	U	R	A	M	E	A	K	E	A	P	L	E	S	Y	C
L	I	O	O	P	A	N	C	A	K	E	S	T	O	F	P
P	T	A	N	C	A	K	E	S	E	H	O	C	A	S	L
M	S	R	S	H	M	A	L	T	U	M	P	L	E	P	S

Page 58-59

Outta My Way, Noway!

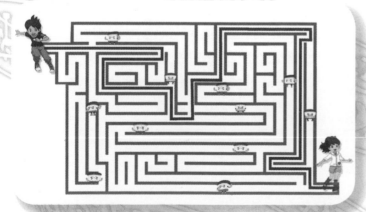

Page 60 Crazy Close-ups

1) **VENOCT**   5) **WAZZAT**

2) **MANJIMUTT**   6) **NEGATIBUZZ**

3) **NOKO**   7) **WIGLIN**

4) **KOMAJIRO**

Page 61 Crossword Crackdown!

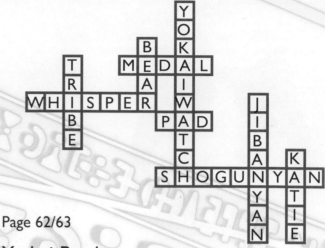

Page 62/63

Yo-kai Battles

BATTLE 1:

KOMASAN VS. KOMAJIRO
WINNER: KOMAJIRO

Though they have almost the same stats, Komajiro takes the win with his resourcefulness. But don't worry these country boys are still the best of brothers!

BATTLE 2:

TATTLETELL VS. HIDABAT
WINNER: HIDABAT

Hidabat shows Tattletell that when you have no friends there aren't many secrets to tell.

BATTLE 3:

JIBANYAN VS. MANJIMUTT
WINNER: JIBANYAN

Not much of a match, as Jibanyan easily overwhelms Manjimutt with his Paws of Fury.

BATTLE 4:

BLAZION VS. WALKAPPA
WINNER: BLAZION

Walkappa tries to spread the love, but in the end, Blazion's quick thinking helps him win. Walkappa's plate, his source of energy, is quickly dried out, and he is unable to continue.

Page 66

Word Detective

Here are 30 words you can make, but there are many more.

achy	itchy	two
await	oak	wacky
away	oath	what
cat	okay	whit
chat	tack	why
city	taco	wick
coat	thaw	witch
cow	thick	with
hack	tick	yacht
hawk	tock	yak

Page 70-71

Seek and Find

ANNUAL COLLECTORS CHALLENGE ANSWERS

1) Mt Wildwood

2) Yo-kai Pad

3) Pizza

4) Manjimutt

5) Roughraff

6) Hungramps

7) Blazion

8) Nosirs

9) To become a movie star

10) Hidabat

11) The countryside

12) Fidgephant

13) Komasan

14) Dismarelda

15) Keep his head disc wet

16) Venoct

17) Archer

18) Tattletell

19) Jibanyan

20) Katie

21) Blazion

22) Noway

23) Negatibuzz

24) Insomni

25) Espy

26) Shady Tribe

27) Happierre

28) Jibanyan

29) Shogunyan

30) Sheen

31) He gets arrested by the police

32) Robonyan

33) Dismarelda

34) Chocobars

35) Cheeksqueek

36) B3-NK1